## WRITTEN BY
CHRISTINE LAZIER AND MARIE FARRÉ,
BÉATRICE FONTANEL, PATRICK GEISTDORFER, ANDRE LUCAS,
PIERRE PFEFFER, BERNARD PLANCHE, PENNY STANLEY-BAKER

## COVER DESIGN BY
STEPHANIE BLUMENTHAL

## TRANSLATED AND ADAPTED BY
PAULA SCHANILEC AND ROSEMARY WALLNER

**PUBLISHED BY CREATIVE EDUCATION**
123 South Broad Street, Mankato, Minnesota 56001
Creative Education is an imprint of The Creative Company

**Library of Congress Cataloging-in-Publication Data**
[Animaux sauvages. English]
Exotic wildlife / by Christine Lazier et al. ; [illustrated by Joële Boucher et al. ;
translated and adapted by Paula Schanilec and Rosemary Wallner].
(Creative Discoveries)
Includes index.
Summary: A brief look at a wide variety of exotic animal species such as monkeys, elephants, and jungle cats.
ISBN: 0-88682-956-9
1. Animals—Miscellanea—Juvenile literature. [1. Animals—Miscellanea.]
I. Lazier, Christine. II. Boucher, Joële, ill. III. Title. IV. Series.
QL49.A613                                                                    1999
590—dc21                                                                97-27530

First edition

2  4  6  8  9  7  5  3  1

# EXOTIC WILDLIFE

**CONTENTS**

**CREATIVE EDUCATION**

# Polar bears live in the icy Arctic.

You are not likely to encounter the animals in this book—at least not in the wild. Many live in remote areas: in the frozen tundra, the jungle, or the sea. People are a threat to wild animals. Many have become rare or endangered. By reading about these animals, you can begin to learn what they need to survive in our world.

Let's begin with a visit to the Arctic, the frozen, windswept continent around the North Pole.

**Polar bears are determined hunters.** They have to be. Food is scarce in the Arctic. Yet polar bears eat a tremendous amount. Polar bears can weigh as much as 1,543 pounds (700 kg), and a male can weigh three times as much as a full-grown lion.

Polar bears prey mainly on seals and walruses. They lie in wait on the ice and catch seals when they come up to the surface to breathe.

**Baby polar bears are born in a cubbing den.** The female digs a cave, or den, under the snow just before her cubs are born. She stays there with the cubs until they grow bigger and stronger. At birth, cubs are the size of a rat and weigh about one pound (0.45 kg). But they grow quickly on their mother's milk, which is full of fat. By the time they are three months old, they weigh 22 pounds (10 kg) and can go outside.

In March or April the mother takes her cubs out and teaches them to hunt for baby seals. The young cubs stay with their mother for another year or so. Then, like other polar bears, they live alone, except to mate in the summer.

When seals are scarce, polar bears eat walrus pups, fish, berries, grasses, or seaweed.

Polar bears also hunt Arctic foxes, walruses, and reindeer.

**Polar bears have Arctic equipment.** They are well-protected by a warm fur coat, and, under that, a thick layer of fat. They can swim for hours in the frozen seas. The underside of their paws is covered with hair, which gives them a good grip on the ice so they can walk and run on it without slipping.

**Polar bears may come to town.** In winter, while the pregnant females stay in their dens, the males search for food and may follow the seals southward. The bears may pursue the smell of food right up to someone's doorstep, where they are not welcome! They are usually trapped, tranquilized, and airlifted by helicopter back to the ice.

# Seals live in the cold waters of the northern seas.

**Seals are excellent swimmers,** but they are mammals, like humans. Although they can stay underwater for a long time, they have to come to the surface to breathe. In winter, they make breathing holes in the ice.

**There are many species in the seal family.** Hooded seals have a sac, or a pocket, on their heads. When they are excited, the pocket fills up with air and their heads nearly double in size. Hooded seals can weigh up to 800 pounds (360 kg).

Hooded seals

Ringed seals are much smaller than hooded seals. They stay around or under the coastal ice and eat shellfish and small fish.

**Walruses live on land and in the sea.** Like seals, they give birth to their cubs on land, but they get most of their food from the ocean. They are covered with short, sleek fur. You can recognize walruses by their long tusks.

Walruses

**Their tusks are survival tools.** Walrus tusks are actually two long teeth. These powerful animals use their teeth as clamps to help them climb onto ice floes. They also use their teeth to dig holes in the ice, to scrape the seabed for shellfish, and even to fight with other walruses.

# The emperor penguin rules Antarctica.

**Emperor penguins are devoted fathers.** In early winter when the female has laid her egg, she carefully passes it to the male. He puts it on his feet and covers it with a special fold of skin to keep it warm. Then the female sets off across the ice, back to the sea. The father incubates the egg for 64 days and looks after the young chick. He does not need to eat during the entire incubation time. Instead, he lives off the fat reserves that he has stored in his body.

Seals, sea lions, elephant seals, penguins and other birds live in Antarctica

When the chick is about two months old, its mother returns with a crop full of fish for it. Now the father leaves for the sea, where he recovers and feeds. He has lost one-third of his body weight and is weak. He too returns with food for the chick. When both parents are away, the chicks huddle together in a group until they are big enough to journey to the sea and find food for themselves.

Brown bears can be found all over the world. They live in North America, Europe, and Asia. One of the largest brown bears is the Kodiak, which lives in Alaska. The males weigh up to 1,500 pounds (680 kg). Grizzlies are also a member of the brown bear species.

**You are not likely to run into a brown bear.** They try to avoid people and other animals, even each other. Males and females live apart, except for a short time each year in the spring when they come together to mate.

**Brown bears are not fussy eaters.** They are omnivores, which means they eat almost anything—plants, nuts, insects, grubs, fish, honey, and young animals. They eat all summer to store up fat, then sleep, or hibernate, through the winter.

# Grizzlies are powerful and protective.

A young grizzly's first fight with a caribou

**The huge grizzly deserves respect.** When this big brown bear stands on its hind legs, it may be 10 feet (3 m) tall—higher than a room's ceiling! They are called grizzlies because their fur often turns a grizzled gray color, and they can be fierce. Like most bears, grizzlies do not like to mix with people, but they do not normally attack humans. People must use caution in grizzly territory, however, because grizzlies attack if they are surprised or if people threaten their food or their cubs.

A grizzly bear raids a bees' nest for honey. The bear's thick fur protects it from the stings of the angry bees.

**Grizzlies patrol their territory.** They live in the mountains and forests of Alaska, Canada, and northern Siberia. Each bear has its own territory where it returns year after year. It patrols this stretch of land, scratching on trees and leaving its scent. These "keep out" signals warn other grizzlies to stay away.

Grizzlies eat berries and small animals such as squirrels, but they'll attack caribou and bighorn sheep too. They can kill large animals with several powerful blows.

They hide the prey under trees and return to eat it later. Sometimes they chase bison, but since bison can run faster than a grizzly, these bears prefer to hunt young or wounded animals.

# Black bears are smaller than brown bears.

**Bears must forage for food in the wilderness.** In some of the national parks in the United States, black bears got so used to eating people's food that they forgot how to find food on their own. They raided garbage cans or took handouts from tourists. This became a problem because the bears lost their natural fear of humans. Now park officials warn tourists and campers never to feed a bear, and the park staffs use bear-proof garbage containers.

Black bears prowl for food. Wise campers hang their food from a tree to protect it from animals.

**Look at the bear's huge paws!** Bears walk and run on all fours. They have broad flat paws, like human feet. Each paw has five long, curved claws which can be terrible weapons. A bear can run about 22 miles (35 km) per hour; you have to be very fast to outrun a bear.

When it feels threatened, a bear charges its victim and then stands on its hind legs to attack. It swipes its enemy with its front claws.

**Bear cubs are born in the winter** in the warm den their mother digs for them. By spring they are old enough to follow her outside when she hunts for food. She teaches them to dig up roots and to pick berries. She shows them how to open an ants' nest with their claws, to swim and catch fish, and to climb trees to get fruit and raid birds' nests. Many species of brown bear grow too big and heavy to climb trees once the bears become adults.

Bear cubs stay with their mother until they are about 18 months old. Then they must start life on their own.

# Lynx and wolves are at home in prairies and forests.

**Lynx are wild cats.** In Alaska, Canada, and the northern United States, lynx live in forests. But in Asia, Europe, and the southern United States, red lynx live among the rocks, in marshlands, and in deserts.

Lynx are an endangered species.

**The lynx is solitary and nocturnal.** Each lynx marks out its own area with urine and droppings. The animal's scent tells other lynx to keep away. Their dappled fur helps them to hide among the trees and rocks.

Lynx

**Wolverines are strong, ferocious hunters.** They live in northern coniferous forests, and they are so strong they are capable of killing animals larger than themselves. In the winter, wolverines hunt large reindeer and caribou, but they also eat berries.

Wolverine

**Wolves communicate with each other through different cries:** growling, snarling, barking, and howling. When they hunt at night, they howl to contact each other and keep the pack together in the dark.

Wolves are an endangered species in most areas, but they are beginning to make a comeback in Minnesota and Alaska.

**Millions of bison and pronghorn once roamed the prairies of North America,** but early settlers hunted them almost to extinction. Federal laws protect remaining herds that graze in national parks.

Pronghorn

# Animals are hard to spot in the dense Amazon rainforest.

The three-toed sloth spends most of its life hanging upside down at the top of a tree.

The Amazon River flows across South America. On either side stretches a vast tropical rainforest. Walking through it, a person may think it is uninhabited, but in fact there are thousands of animals all around.

The rainforest is hot and damp. Many trees grow as high as a 10-story building.

Thousands of animals live in the rainforest, but they are hard to see because they hide in the trees.

**Jaguars are the largest cats in South America.** They weigh more than 440 pounds (200 kg). Young learn to hunt with their mother, hiding in the shadows and pouncing on their prey. Sometimes they climb trees and attack sleeping monkeys or birds.

**Jaguars and humans hunt the endangered ocelot.** Although many countries no longer allow the sale of ocelot skins, hunters sometimes illegally kill ocelots for their beautiful coats. Boa constrictors and caimans (alligator-like creatures) often kill the cubs. When a male and female ocelot walk together through the forest, they meow to each other like domesticated cats. They are sometimes known as "tiger cats" or "jaguar cats."

Ocelot

**A peccary is a small wild boar with skinny legs.** They live in packs of up to 100 pigs. Each animal has a special gland on its bottom that produces an oily secretion. They recognize each other's smell and use their own smell to mark their territory. When a peccary is attacked, it chatters its teeth. The noise it makes is so loud that it can be heard far away.

Peccary

# Tribes of small monkeys leap from tree to tree.

The steamy, leafy tropical rainforest is the kingdom of the small monkeys. They leap among the treetops in noisy, chattering clans.

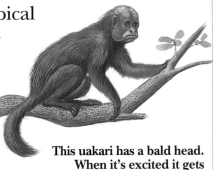

This uakari has a bald head. When it's excited it gets red in the face.

Woolly monkeys are tamed for pets.

Marmoset

**Squirrel monkeys chase each other through the trees.** Quick and agile, they appear and vanish among the branches as if by magic.

**The pygmy marmoset is the smallest monkey in the world.** You could easily fit one into your pocket. It grips the trees with tiny, curved claws.

Golden lion tamarins are very rare.

Night monkey

Monkeys use their long tails to help them balance, which is why they do not fall out of the trees.

The night monkey is the only monkey that stays awake at night. Its enormous eyes help it to see in the dark.

Squirrel monkeys

**Snakes poison their prey or suffocate it by squeezing it so it can't breathe.**

**A tree boa is well camouflaged.** With its emerald green skin and white stripes, you would not notice this snake among the leaves. It lies very still, waiting to attack a bird or lizard. Like other boas, it coils itself around its victim, then suffocates it by squeezing it until it stops breathing.

Scarlet macaw

A rattlesnake kills with a poisonous bite. Its fangs inject venom into its prey. Rattlesnakes swallow their food whole.

**Anacondas are one of the world's longest snakes.** They can be nearly 30 feet (9 m) long. They lurk in rivers and attack animals that come there to drink.

A female can give birth to 30 or 40 live young in one litter.

A jaguar prowls by the river. It will even attack the sharp-toothed caiman. The bird-eating spider is also on the lookout for prey.

Red ibis

Toucan

Jacamar

Jacamar

**South American macaws are the most colorful parrots in the world.** The scarlet macaw is also one of the world's largest birds. Parrots live in large, noisy flocks, except when it is time to mate.

Anaconda

**The toucan's large beak is full of holes,** which makes it lightweight. The beak is made of a bony substance that is hard and colorful on the outside. Although their beaks are enormous, toucans use them skillfully to pick fruit and to catch lizards, frogs, and small chicks.

Some birds chase insects high in the trees, but the jacamar perches on a low branch and waits for moths and butterflies. The bird snatches its dinner from the air and hits it against a branch to kill it.

**The red ibis is prized for its beautiful feathers.** Although it is protected by law, people still hunt this bird. But the biggest threat to it and all the animals of the rainforest is the destruction of the forest itself. As people chop down the trees, birds and animals lose their food and shelter.

# Life is harsh in the high mountains of the Andes.

**Mountains are inhospitable places.** The higher you climb, the colder and windier it gets. The air is thinner—there is less oxygen for plants and animals to breathe. Only a few small plants can grow here. Amazingly, many kinds of animals live in the high Andes Mountains of South America. They include insects, birds, vicuñas, and guanacos. Lower down, in the warm, wet forests, live many other animals such as the spectacled bear.

Alpaca
Llama
Vicuña

**Vicuñas, guanacos, alpacas, and llamas are related to camels.** They are smaller than camels, and because their feet are narrower and firmer, they can walk on steep mountainous trails. People now raise llamas and alpacas for their long, woolly hair.

**No two spectacled bears look alike!** Each has a different pattern of white fur around its eyes. This gentle animal lives on its own or with its family. It eats mainly fruit such as figs and the young shoots of palm trees. It feeds at night and sleeps during the day in a nest built from broken branches. Spectacled bears are very wary of people for good reasons: people have cut down trees, destroying their habitat, and they have hunted the bears for attacking llamas. Spectacled bears are now an endangered species. Only a few thousand of them are left in the world.

**Watch out for the guanaco's spit!**
Guanaco
Guanacos live in small groups. In the mating season, the males fight fiercely over the females. They get very excited and spit a mixture of saliva and stomach juices into each other's faces.

**Vicuñas live 13,000 feet (4,000 m) high.** They live in family groups of a male with several females and their young. The male marks out their territory with his urine and droppings. In spring, each female has a baby. When a young male is a year old, he joins a group of other young males. Three years later, when he is an adult, he wanders off alone to look for his own females.

Long ago, the Incas hunted the vicuñas. Only the emperor of the Incas was allowed to wear a cape of vicuña wool. Today, vicuñas are a protected species.

# Pumas and condors hunt their prey from above.

**The puma is a strong and agile mountain cat.** It likes to perch on a rocky peak and wait for its unsuspecting prey to pass below. Then it pounces. Pumas, also called mountain lions or cougars, hunt young stags, guanacos, rabbits, coyotes, and lynx. Pumas are so strong they can carry an animal up to five times their own weight. They also catch large insects, snakes, and sometimes even fish.

The female puma is pregnant for three months. Before giving birth, she looks for a sheltered place at the bottom of a cliff to deliver and raise her cubs. She feeds them her milk, and when they are two and a half months old, she begins teaching them to hunt. When they are a year or two old, they leave her to live on their own. Pumas are endangered.

**The condor is a huge bird of prey that is now endangered. It soars by day in the wind among the peaks of the Andes. It swoops down onto young or wounded llamas, goats, and lambs. Mostly, however, it eats the flesh of dead mammals.**

# The grasslands of Africa are a paradise for large mammals.

African savannas are large plains with few trees and plenty of grass—when it rains. Many large mammals live here: antelope, giraffes, buffalo, and elephants.

**Elephants are the largest animals that walk the earth.** Some adult males are as tall as the first story of a house.

Elephants are the heaviest animals that live on land—one elephant can weigh as much as 100 adult humans! But even though they are very big, elephants move gently and quietly.

With their colossal size, their strength, and their wisdom, they live without fear. What would dare to attack them? Even a hunting lion moves out of their way. Elephants eat plants and attack other living creatures only when they feel threatened.

# An elephant's trunk can do almost everything.

The African elephant is larger than the Indian elephant.

**Elephants spend all day—and most of the night—eating.** In fact, they sleep for only about four hours a day! A full-grown elephant can eat 330 pounds (150 kg) of leaves, grass, fruit, and roots a day. Sometimes they push over a whole tree just to reach the leaves. They often eat soil to get the minerals they need, and they have to drink a lot of water too—19 to 24 gallons (70 to 90 L) each day!

**What is a tool, a hand, a pump, a snorkel, and a nose all in one?** An elephant's trunk! It is made of muscle and has no bones. It is hollow and ends at the elephant's lips. An elephant uses its trunk to breathe, to pick fruit, and to throw a lion into the air! It can drink and shower itself with water—a great delight in the hot sun. It lifts its trunk in the air to sniff out danger and water. And, if an elephant swims underwater, it can hold its trunk above the surface to breathe.

**It is a trumpet too.** When an elephant calls out, you can hear it for miles around!

## Walking for water

For many months of the year, there is no rain and the grasslands become very dry. Then the elephants move toward the forest, where there are always leaves to eat and water to drink. Once the rains come, the elephants move back onto the plains where fresh green grass has begun to grow.

An elephant can easily walk 19 miles (30 km) a day, plodding along on its enormous thick-skinned feet.

# Elephants have sensitive skins and strong tusks.

**Did you know that elephants have thin, sensitive skin?** Sharp grasses scratch them; tsetse flies and ticks bite them and suck their blood.

To protect themselves, elephants roll in mud. As the mud dries, it cakes into a protective armor. Sometimes elephants spray themselves with dust as well. A little bird called a tickbird helps by picking off the pests and eating them.

**What are tusks for?** Elephants can use their tusks for fighting, but they are also used for taking the bark off of trees, grubbing up roots, and digging into damp sand to find drinking water. Giraffes, rhinos, and other animals share the water the elephants find.

Elephants are usually either right-tusked or left-tusked! Their tusks grow all their lives, and can be nearly 10 feet (3 m) long and weigh more than 220 pounds (100 kg). If one of the tusks crumbles or breaks, it can become infected. An infected tusk is very painful and makes the elephant aggressive.

**An elephant has strong teeth.** It has four flat molars for grinding up the plants it eats. As one tooth wears down, a new tooth pushes through to replace it. In all, an elephant has six sets of teeth. Each tooth weighs around 11 pounds (5 kg) and is about one and a half feet (50 cm) long!

Elephants use their tusks to dig for water.

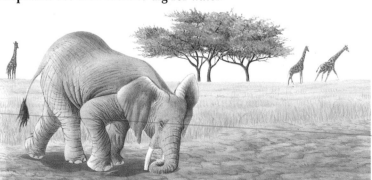

# A baby elephant is born.

**A 265-pound (120-kg) baby**

After a pregnancy of nearly two years, the mother clears a private spot to give birth. Other female elephants come to help.

The mother dries her newborn baby and cuddles it with her trunk. Then she kicks the baby gently to help it stand up, lifting it with her trunk.

The other females of the herd sniff the new baby to get to know it.

A baby does not use its trunk for the first few months, so it reaches for its mother's nipples with its mouth. It can drink 2.3 gallons (10 L) of milk a day.

**Cuddled, pampered, and protected**

When it is only two days old, the baby elephant can walk along with the other elephants. It holds its mother's tail so it doesn't get lost. The herd protects it and the baby suckles from other females as well as its mother. The elephants help it to cross rivers and to climb hills by supporting it around the middle with their trunks.

**Young elephants grow quickly.** The baby feeds from its mother for about a year. When it is three months old it also starts to eat adult food. The baby learns how to use its trunk to pull up grass and pick acacia fruit. Until its own teeth are strong enough, the mother mashes the grass and leaves before putting them in the baby's mouth. Young male elephants stay with the herd until they are about 10 years old. Females stay all their lives.

**The leader of the herd is the oldest female.** Every herd is a large family made up of the head female, her sisters and daughters, and their children of all ages. The leader is the oldest and the wisest. She knows where to find food at different seasons of the year and where to find water. She also knows where there is danger.

The other females learn from her and follow wherever she goes. When she dies, the next oldest female in the herd takes over as the leader.

**Elephants are affectionate to each other.** They never quarrel. They touch and stroke each other with their trunks. Each elephant has its own place in the herd. Although elephants push against each other, they only pretend to fight. If a baby elephant is upset, a female puts the end of her trunk into its mouth to comfort it.

**Elephants are noisy eaters.** As they eat, they make gurgling noises that sound like the rumblings human stomachs sometimes make. This "concerto" allows them to keep in touch when they can't see each other. They also make other sounds too low for humans to hear.

# People must protect the elephants.

**Warning!** A female elephant sounds the alarm, trumpeting loudly through her trunk. She has spotted a lion. The others squeeze close together in a circle with the babies in the middle. The lead elephant pulls tufts of grass and throws them at the lion. Then she moves forward, ears flapping and tusks forward.

**Male elephants live in small groups.** When they are about 10 years old, young males begin to get on the females' nerves, and so they leave their mother's herd. At first they join a group of other young males, but as they get older, they go off on their own. At mating time, a male elephant gets very excited. A thick, smelly liquid runs down his chceks from a gland between his ears and eyes. He follows a female until she allows him to mate with her.

Male elephants fight to test their strength, but, like humans, they gather around to help the sick and dying. Even after an elephant has died, the others try to help it stand up.

People still kill clephants for their ivory tusks even though it has been illegal to sell or buy ivory since 1989. The loss of forests and grasslands also threatens elephants.

# Zebras, buffalo, and warthogs also live on the African plains.

**Zebras live in constant danger.** Their stripes help to disguise them as they graze among the shrubs, but they are prey to lions, hyenas, leopards, and cheetahs. They can't go more than three days without drinking water, and leopards often wait for them to come and drink at a water hole.

Zebras live in family groups, a male with his females and their young. When the male is 16 to 18 years old, a younger male pushes him out of the group and takes his place.

Antelope

**Buffalo are Africa's wild cattle.** They can be fierce. They can charge a lion and rip it open with their horns. But when an elephant chases them, they gallop away as fast as they can! Buffalo are said to be irritable and dangerous, but they will not charge unless injured.

**Have you ever heard hyenas laugh?** It means they have found some exciting prey. Hyenas are the scavengers of the African grasslands. They feed on dead animal carcasses, but when in a group, they will also attack live animals.

**What a strange animal a warthog is!** Its head is covered with warts. It has two long canine teeth that stick up on either side of its snout. These are useful for digging up roots, bulbs, and tubers to eat.

The warthog also eats grass, fruit, bark, and sometimes catches small rodents. It makes its home in an abandoned burrow or in an old termite or porcupine nest. When it is threatened, it sticks up its tail and runs away with its family close behind!

Warthog

# The giraffe looks down from a great height!

**A giraffe's long neck makes drinking difficult.** To drink, a giraffe has to spread its front legs wide apart, then swing its neck up and down, faster and faster, until its mouth reaches the water. It drinks 16 quarts (15 L) of water at a time.

**A giraffe can see for miles around.** Because it is almost 20 feet (6 m) tall, it can see a lion creeping through the grass long before the antelope, zebras, and other grassland animals are aware of the predator's presence.

**A giraffe spends half the day eating.** It munches leaves, small branches, pods, and acacia fruit. It finds the tastiest morsels by looking and smelling. The giraffe, which can reach even the highest branches of many trees, feels for the softest fruit with its sensitive, hairy lips. Its black tongue, covered in slime, reaches through the branches to find soft twigs. The inside of its mouth is hard, so sharp thorns cannot hurt it.

**Giraffes watch out for each other.** They often graze in small groups, each giraffe scanning a different part of the horizon on the lookout for enemies.

**A giraffe gives birth standing up** . . . and her baby falls more than six feet (2 m) to the ground! The mother then licks the baby to dry and rouse it. After an hour, the baby rises on its wobbly legs and follows its mother onto the grassland. It grows by more than three feet (1 m) in its first year.

# Rhinos love to wallow in mud.

**Insects are their enemies.** A rhino's skin is thick, hard, and rough, but it will do almost anything to avoid being stung by an insect! That is why it spends most of the day wallowing in muddy waters. When it gets out, the mud dries hard on its hide; insects cannot sting through this dirty shield!

A rhinoceros weighs about 4,000 pounds (2 metric tons). Although it looks slow and heavy, it can run at 31 miles (50 km) per hour. Its horn is made of keratin, just like people's hair and nails.

**Rhinos live in small groups.** Rhinos mark their territory with urine and droppings. If an unknown male strays onto another's land, he is immediately chased away.

Rhinos feed on the leaves of small bushes. They always follow the same route and make a useful path for other animals through thorn bushes.

Rhinos are born without horns. A baby weighs a hefty 88 pounds (40 kg) at birth. It drinks its mother's milk for a year or so and stays with her until her next calf is born.

Humans hunt the endangered rhinoceros for its valuable horns.

The mother looks after her baby for two to three years. She protects it from hyenas.

# Fierce, strong males rule tribes of baboons.

Baboons are strong and aggressive. Their long, dog-like muzzles and sharp teeth make them fierce fighters. They live in big groups, or tribes, under the leadership of a dominant male. Lookouts are posted to warn the group of danger.

## Living in a baboon tribe

The strongest males lead the other males, the females, and their offspring. They rule the group and defend it against any threat. When they see a leopard, lion, or hyena, they bark loudly to warn others in the tribe.

**Baboons are omnivores, meaning they eat almost anything.** They eat plants, lizards, insects, worms, scorpions, and eggs. Baboons will even devour newborn gazelles and antelope.

**The birth of a baby is a big event.** All the members of the baboon tribe want to stroke the baby! They treat the mother with great respect. The dominant male comes and sits next to her.

At first, baby baboons stay close to their mothers. After three months they begin playing with their friends.

At eight months, the baby leaves its mother, but she continues to protect it until it is two years old.

As soon as it is born, a baby baboon can cling to its mother's fur and suckle her milk.

Babies cling to the fur on their mothers' bellies; the mothers carry them everywhere.

When they are toddlers, they ride on their mothers' backs.

Baboons sometimes try to catch young antelope.

# On the grasslands of Africa, the lion is king.

**The lion tells everyone how important he is.** At dusk, as the last rays of sunshine turn everything red, the lion's roar is heard across the savanna. He roars so loudly that he can be heard five miles (8 km) away. He may roar to show off his strength or to express his pleasure after a good meal.

**Lions live in a family group.** The pride is made up of two or three related males with their females and cubs. There may be up to 30 lions in a pride.

Male lions patrol their territory and chase away lions from other prides. Females are in charge of caring for the young and hunting.

**Lions are said to be very lazy.** They sleep about 20 hours a day. When they rest, they lie against each other and yawn or snooze. Often, they lick themselves or rub their muzzles as they lie in the shade.

**At sunrise or sunset, the lionesses set off to hunt.** They look for easy prey among a herd of zebras, gnus, antelope, or gazelle. They catch an old or weak animal that cannot run as fast as the others.

The lioness has to leave behind her cubs when she hunts. One or two lionesses may stay back to baby-sit, because if all the adults leave, the cubs are in danger of attack—especially from hyenas.

# The lioness teaches her cubs to hunt.

## A perfectly planned attack
Lions are not fast runners, so they tend to hunt as a team. When they find prey, they surround it and creep up until they are close enough to attack. Then they pounce.

## The lion's share
The male lions are the first to eat, then the females take a turn. Finally, the cubs are allowed to join in. Sometimes a cub is accidentally killed in the scuffle for food.

**Lion cubs love to play and hunt.** Three months after mating, the lioness gives birth to two or three brown-spotted cubs. They suckle from their mother or one of her sisters until they are six months old. At three months they start eating meat.

The lioness teaches her cubs how to hunt when they are about eight months old. She captures a small animal, lets it loose near the cubs, and patiently lets them chase and catch it.

**In ancient times, lions were found in many parts of Europe, Asia, and Africa.** The remaining Asian lions live in India's Gir Forest. Lions can still be found in east and central Africa, but most live on reserves—protected from hunters. Some reserves have hospitals for treating wounded and sick animals. Lions also reside in national parks and zoos, where they can live up to 25 years. In the wild, they live eight to 10 years.

The lioness teaches her cubs to hunt.

**Look out for the leopard above your head!** During the day they sprawl along large branches. As they rest they keep an eye on their territory below. At dusk they spring to the ground and prowl through the bushes looking for prey: baboons, gazelles, hares, and even lizards or snakes.

Cheetah

**Leopards will attack anything!** Young monkeys, especially those that have strayed from their group, are common prey. Leopards sometimes sneak into villages and attack lambs, chickens, and dogs. They also kill warthogs and antelope twice their own size.

## One killing bite
Like other big cats, a leopard leaps on its prey and bites into its soft neck to strangle it. The prey cannot breathe and quickly dies. If the corpse is too big to eat all at once, the leopard drags it up into a tree, out of the way of jackals, hyenas, and lions. It returns later to finish its meal.

**Big cats are prey to people.** Most of the big cats, including leopards and cheetahs, are endangered. Hunting and wilderness destruction are to blame. Concerned groups are working hard to protect them.

**Have you heard of a caracal?** It looks like a small lynx but has yellow, fawn-colored, or reddish fur. It hunts hares, gazelles, and small antelope.

It lies in wait in the trees, or on a high rock, and then leaps. A caracal is so quick it can catch a bird in flight. It can even overpower an eagle!

Caracal

# Cheetahs are the fastest animals on land.

**Cheetahs are built for speed.** They have small heads, flexible backs, and long, powerful back legs. They are the only cats whose claws do not retract into their paws. Instead, their claws act like the studs on running shoes, gripping the ground as they run.

**A cheetah's top speed is 68.2 miles (110 km) per hour,** but it can maintain that speed for just a few seconds. If it doesn't catch its prey within 219 yards (200 m), it must give up.

**Females live separately from the males** in small groups with their cubs. When the cubs are young, their mother hides them before she goes hunting. When she returns she feeds them with meat she has already chewed.

The mother cheetah keeps her cubs close to the trees, so they can quickly climb away from danger.

# Crocodiles, hippos, and brightly colored birds . . .

The Nile is the longest river in the world, but Africa also has other mighty rivers. They flow through deserts, jungles, and grasslands. Many animals come to the rivers to drink. But beware. A crocodile may be lying in wait beneath the murky surface!

**River birds find plenty to eat.** Herons, egrets, and ibis catch frogs, fish, and insects. Geese and ducks graze on the grass. Migrating birds, such as storks and some teals, spend the winter in Africa.

**A hippo's eyes, ears, and nostrils are all on the top of its head,** so it can see, hear, and breathe without getting out of the water. A hippo has special valves that block off its ears and nostrils when it dives. Hippos spend all day in the river avoiding the scorching heat of the sun.

**Hippos feed only at night.** When the sun goes down, the hippos wade out of the water and graze on the land. A hippo can eat 88 pounds (40 kg) of grass a night. You can see where they have been by the trail of droppings left behind!

**What teeth!** When a male hippo yawns, he is not tired. He is showing off his strong teeth to other males. Hippos fight fiercely over females and, as a result, they are often covered with scars.

**Baby hippos are born underwater,** and the mother helps her baby come up to the surface to breathe. The baby suckles underwater but rides on its mother's back when she is swimming. At six months old, the baby hippo joins its mother to feed on the riverbank.

**Don't go swimming where the hippos wallow!** They may bite you with their long, razor-sharp teeth.

A male controls a group of females, and he does not like people to go near them. Females will chase people if they think their young are in danger. Hippos look clumsy on land, but they move easily and gracefully in the water.

# Crocodiles date back to the age of the dinosaurs.

**Don't be fooled by a crocodile!** They often look fast asleep, but they can be deadly fierce. Crocodiles live beside lakes and rivers in Africa, Asia, Australia, and parts of North and South America. At one time you could find crocodiles in rivers all over Africa, but people have hunted so many for their skins that they have become scarce.

**Crocodiles are reptiles** like snakes, tortoises, and lizards. They have dry, scaly skin, and they lay eggs on land. Crocodiles have several relatives: alligators, caimans, and gavials.

**You can identify a crocodile by its large fourth tooth,** which sticks out on each side of the lower jaw even when its powerful jaws are closed.

**They are the most powerful reptiles in the world.** Crocodiles have existed since the time of the dinosaurs. The noise they make is called a bellow, though it sounds more like a groan. Did you know that there are some crocodiles four times as big as you, and more than 40 times heavier?

**A crocodile's skin is as tough as armor.** It is made of scales, but it is not stiff like a turtle's shell. These scales fit beside each other, and the skin moves and bends easily.

**A crocodile's weapons** are its powerful tail and strong jaws. A crocodile has 54 teeth. They fall out regularly, but new teeth immediately replace the old ones.

A crocodile swims by moving its tail. Only its eyes, ears, and nostrils show above the water.

# Crocodiles are cunning hunters.

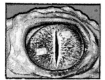

In daylight | At night

A crocodile can see at night like a cat. The pupils of its eyes get wider in the dark.

Crocodiles swallow pebbles, which help to break up the food it has gulped down.

**On land, crocodiles crawl, trot, or sometimes glide** on wet grass, pushing themselves along with their tail. If you ever find yourself being chased by a crocodile, run in zigzags. A crocodile can't turn easily, and this slows it down.

A dozen crocodiles can kill and eat a hippo.

**One meal may last a crocodile a long time.** If it has to, a crocodile can go for two or three months without eating.

**What other animals do crocodiles attack?** Young crocodiles hunt frogs and fish; adults hunt buffalo, zebras, and gazelle. Sometimes they even attack elephants, but they only manage to bite their trunks. When they get old, crocodiles can be eaten by other crocodiles.

**Crocodiles** ambush their prey at the water's edge. A crocodile creeps up on a gazelle drinking from the river, knocks it into the water, and jumps in after it. The crocodile drags the gazelle underwater to drown it, and then twists over and over, tearing off chunks of flesh. A crocodile can't chew, so it swallows the pieces whole.

# Crocodiles cannot live without water.

**Plovers at work**

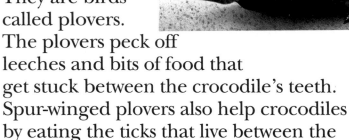

**Crocodiles have strange toothbrushes!** They are birds called plovers. The plovers peck off leeches and bits of food that get stuck between the crocodile's teeth. Spur-winged plovers also help crocodiles by eating the ticks that live between the crocodile's scales.

**A crocodile can stay underwater for two hours** by closing its nostrils so the water cannot get in. A crocodile has a special transparent eyelid to see underwater, and its ears are protected by a thin, waterproof skin that lets only sound through.

**Why do crocodiles sleep in the water?** Like all reptiles, crocodiles lose their body heat when the temperature drops. Because water retains the sun's heat longer than air does, crocodiles spend the night underwater. They crawl out at dawn. Then the sun makes the land warmer than the water, and they lie on the bank basking in the sunshine.

After its meal, a crocodile takes a nap on the bank. If the sun is too hot, it burrows into cool mud or opens its huge mouth to let moisture evaporate from the damp skin inside. This is how the crocodile cools down. If danger threatens, the plovers give a warning cry, and the crocodile quickly dives underwater.

**Each group has its own territory.** Crocodiles usually live in groups. The males mark the boundaries of their territory with a strong-smelling musk. This scent is made in a special gland under their bellies.

The leader has the best spot on the riverbank, the largest number of females, and the largest chunks of meat. Old crocodiles rest on the soft grass, while the younger ones lie on the sloping banks.

# Baby crocodiles live in a nursery.

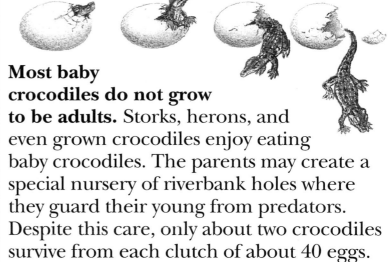

**How are crocodiles hatched?** The mother crocodile uses her front legs to dig a nest shaped like a deep basket. She lays about 40 leathery, white eggs, the size of hens' eggs, and then covers the nest and eggs with sand.

A baby crocodile weighs about one pound (500 g).

**Many animals love to eat crocodiles' eggs!** While the eggs are incubating, the mother seldom leaves the nest. If it is hot, she scurries down to the water for a dip, then lies over the nest to cool it down.

When the eggs are ready to hatch, after about three months, the baby crocodiles call out from inside their eggs. The mother scrapes the sand from the nest, and they break out of their eggs, using a special egg tooth that later drops off. Each baby is about the size of a small lizard.

### The dash for the water
As soon as they hatch, the babies head for the water. They know how to swim right away! Sometimes the mother carries them down to the water in her mouth.

Baby crocodiles eat small worms, snails, and insects.

**Most baby crocodiles do not grow to be adults.** Storks, herons, and even grown crocodiles enjoy eating baby crocodiles. The parents may create a special nursery of riverbank holes where they guard their young from predators. Despite this care, only about two crocodiles survive from each clutch of about 40 eggs.

Mandrills

The hot, wet climate of the equator is just right for a tropical rainforest. The jungle is dense and mysterious. It is difficult to see animals because they are hidden by the thick leaves and branches. Monkeys, apes, and birds live in the trees, while other animals prowl the forest floor.

Drill

de Brazza's monkey

**Is it related to giraffes or zebras?** The okapi looks a bit like a giraffe with a short neck, and it belongs to the same family. But it has the stripes of a zebra. It is shy and easily frightened, running away at the slightest rustle of crushed leaves.

People who lived outside the rainforest didn't know about this animal until the beginning of the 20th century, although local Pygmy tribes had hunted it.

The okapi feeds on young leaves and twigs, buds, and fruit. But it also eats grass, ferns, and mushrooms. Its black tongue is so long it can even lick its own ears and eyes!

A baby okapi grows inside its mother for 14 months before it is born. Then it stays safely hidden in the bushes for two weeks, feeding on its mother's milk. After this, it forages in the forest for food. Only male okapis have horns.

**Giant forest hogs are the largest pigs in Africa.** This wild pig weighs up to 331 pounds (150 kg). Like a warthog, it wallows in mud to keep its skin from drying out and cracking in the sun. Its diet consists of leaves, grass, and fruits.

Giant forest hog

**Bongos are big antelope** which have long, lyre-shaped horns. They are shy and like to live alone. Bongos usually hide in the undergrowth, but they will walk many miles to find their favorite plants and grasses.

**Many different monkeys live in the forest.** The de Brazza's monkey wears a reddish-brown band across its forehead. It is a good climber and swimmer. It also moves quickly and easily on the ground, where it feeds on leaves, fruit, and insects.

When there is danger, they keep still and silent.

Mandrills and drills are baboons. Although both climb well and sleep in trees, they live mainly on the ground. Mandrills have hidden pockets in their cheeks for storing extra food.

In the tropical rainforest, apes swing on long creepers, birds flit among the giant trees, and a flying squirrel leaps from branch to branch.

Hornbill

Chimpanzee

Gray parrot

Flying squirrel

Okapi

Bongo

Congo peacock

# Gorillas are strong but gentle.

## Gorillas can be huge!
They can be three times as heavy as an adult human, but they are gentle giants. They eat only vegetables and leaves, chewing them up with their strong teeth.

Gorillas live in the tropical forests and mountains of Africa, in groups of up to 30. The gorilla is an endangered species, and poaching of them is a problem.

## They nibble all the time.
During the day they walk around the forest, and half the time they are eating leaves, berries, shoots, and even bark. Mountain gorillas feed on wild celeries, thistles, and nettles.

## The oldest male silverback is the leader.
Gorillas are not fully grown until they are 15 years old. Then their black back changes to silver-gray. The leader is strong but kind. He protects the rest of the group.

**Gorilla's foot**

**Gorilla's hand**

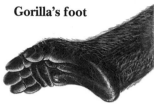

## Baby gorillas are small and helpless.
A newborn gorilla weighs about three pounds (1.5 kg), about half the weight of a human baby. Its mother takes it with her wherever she goes, and it relies on her for everything.

Above, a baby gorilla stays with its mother until it is four years old. Below, older gorillas stay on the look out for danger.

## The baby grows stronger and more active.
When it is about five weeks old, it begins to crawl. By four months it can walk on all fours, and by eight and a half months it can stand upright. Others in the group look after the young gorilla and treat it gently.

The mother teaches her young which plants to eat. Even when they are old enough to look after themselves, the young gorillas stay with the group for many years. When a young male becomes a silverback, he leaves the group and lives on his own until he can find his own territory and females to gather together.

Gorillas are too heavy to swing in the trees, but they are fast and agile on the ground. They curl their hands and walk on their knuckles.

# Chimpanzees are nimble and bright.

You can see what a chimpanzee is feeling from the expression on its face.

**As soon as the sun rises, chimpanzees are searching for food.** Chimpanzees are known for liking bananas, but they can't always find a banana plantation. In the jungle, they eat fruits, buds, nuts, and cereals. Sometimes they catch lizards, insects, and even small monkeys. Chimpanzees are in danger of extinction in the wild.

**Chimpanzees are good at solving problems.** If a chimp is thirsty and far from a stream, it chews up leaves to make a sponge. It pushes the sponge into the forks of branches to soak up water caught there. Then it squeezes the water into its mouth. Sometimes a chimp uses a large leaf like a spoon, dipping it into water and drinking from it as if it were a soup spoon.

Chimpanzees are very fond of termites. They poke long stalks of grass into holes in the termites' nest. The termites climb on, and when the chimp pulls out the stalks, it can lick off the termites.

These chimps have found a termites' nest.

**A fresh nest every night**
Chimpanzees like to build a platform of branches and leaves high in a tree, where they can sleep out of reach of predators. Mothers sleep with their babies; the others sleep alone. Gorillas sleep on the ground in nests of branches padded with leaves.

# Life is hard in the African desert.

Deserts cover most of north and southwest Africa. It is very hot during the day and very cold at night. Rain is rare and food is scarce, so it is surprising how many animals manage to live there.

## Escaping the heat
Lizards bury themselves in the sand and wait for the ants and beetles they eat.

Some lizards shelter in bushes or in the shade of a rock.

Jerboas—jumping rodents—avoid the scorching ground by leaping along on powerful hind legs. Their tails help them keep their balance.

Savanna gazelle

**How do animals drink when there is no water?** Many lizards get enough water from the insects and plants they eat. Jerboas and other rodents get enough from the seeds on which they feed.

Desert antelope like springboks, oryxes, and gazelles can last months without drinking. They survive on dew and sap from plants that they eat.

**Ostriches are the largest birds, but they can't fly.** An ostrich measures nearly 10 feet (3 m) in height and weighs more than 330 pounds (150 kg). They live in the desert and savannas but stay close to water holes because they need to drink. Although ostriches cannot fly, they can run very fast— up to 43 miles (70 km) per hour.

**The male ostrich is a good father.** He lives with several females who all lay their eggs in the same nest. He guards the nest and takes turns with the females sitting on the eggs for 42 days. Each egg weighs about three pounds (1.5 kg). The shell is so thick a person would need a saw to open it. Luckily a baby ostrich has a special egg tooth to help it break out!

# Desert creatures are specially suited to survive the African heat.

Baby ostriches grow almost half an inch (1 cm) a day. As soon as they hatch, they leave the nest and begin to explore. If a hyena or jackal is spotted, the ostrich parents cry loudly, flap their wings, and zigzag around to distract the enemy. Meanwhile, another ostrich rushes the chicks to a safe place.

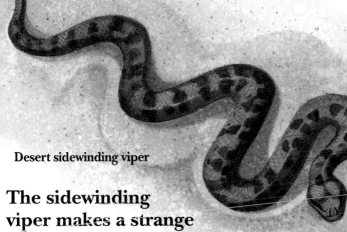

Desert sidewinding viper

**The sidewinding viper makes a strange pattern in the sand.** As it flicks its head and body sideways, hardly any of its belly touches the hot ground for long. It can dive beneath the sand where it waits, coiled up, with just its head showing. If a small rodent passes, the snake shoots out and snatches it. At night, the snake searches for prey among the bushes and burrows.

**The smallest fox of all lives in the desert.** Fennec foxes weigh less than 3.5 pounds (1.5 kg). They have big, sensitive ears that give them acute hearing. The soles of their feet are covered with protective hair so they can walk on the sand without getting burned. In daytime they tend to remain inside their cool burrows, and at night they go out hunting for rodents, lizards, birds, and insects.

**Oryxes, like sidewinding vipers and fennecs, are nocturnal.** During the mating season, male oryxes fight noisy duels using their long, thin horns. After mating, females go to the scrub at the edge of the desert to give birth. They give birth during the rainy season, when there is plenty of water available for their babies to drink.

The oryx, an endangered animal, can tolerate very high temperatures.

**Oryxes can walk miles to find water.** But, like many desert animals, they need little to drink and they hardly sweat at all. They graze at night on succulent desert plants whose fruits or bulbs provide them with the moisture they need.

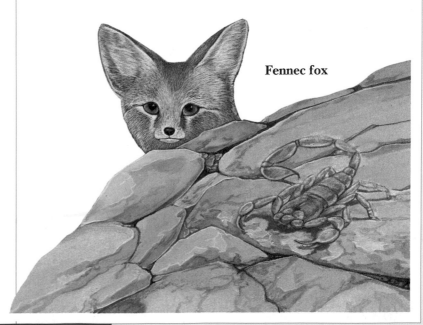

Fennec fox

# Giant pandas live in China.

Snow leopards and pandas live in the high mountains of the Himalayas. In the tropical rain-forests of Southeast Asia are the orangutan and the tiger. All of these animals are shy and keep to themselves.

## One of the rarest animals

Giant pandas are related to a long-tailed mammal that is in turn related to the rac-coon. Giant pandas are in danger of dying out, but scientists have been trying for many years to breed them in captivity.

## A diet of bamboo

Bamboo is the giant panda's staple diet. They bite off the bark with their teeth and carefully strip off the leaves with their front paws. They eat the leaves and suck the sweet juice inside the soft shoots. A sort of sixth finger acts like a thumb, helping them to hold the tiniest twig.

**Giant pandas spend half their lives feeding.** They have to eat 12 hours a day to get the 26 pounds (12 kg) of bamboo they need. They also eat flowers like gentians, irises, and crocuses. Sometimes they feed on dead rats. When they are full, they climb into a tree to rest.

**Giant pandas are shy and usually live on their own in the forest.** But in spring they are ready to mate. The males call out to attract a female. Sometimes two males will fight each other for the attention of the same female. A male and female spend a day or two together, getting to know each other, before they mate.

# Giant pandas are an endangered species.

Giant panda mothers are as cuddly as they look. Four or five months after mating, the female giant panda gives birth in the fork of a tree. She can only look after one baby at a time, so if she has twins, she abandons the weaker one. For three months, until the baby learns to walk, the mother carries it with her wherever she goes. She rocks it and licks it tenderly and caresses it when it cries. She keeps it safe from leopards and wolves.

**Baby giant pandas love playing.** They slide down slopes, turn somersaults, and hang upside down in trees. By the time they are a month old, they have their black "socks, glasses, and jacket"!

Young giant pandas start eating bamboo shoots when they are six months old, but continue to drink their mother's milk for another two months.

**There are fewer than 1,000 giant pandas left in the wild.** As their territory gets smaller and smaller, there is less for them to eat. People are destroying bamboo forests to make fields for crops and to build villages. Giant pandas cannot move to new territory because people have taken over most places. There is an effort to protect giant pandas, but unless something is done to save their habitat, the only place to find a giant panda may be at the zoo.

# A leopard that loves the snow

**The snow leopard has a luxurious coat to keep out the bitter cold.** It lives up to 19,685 feet (6,000 m) high among the frozen peaks of the Himalayas in Asia where there is snow all year round. Its magnificent coat is very thick, especially in winter.

You can recognize a snow leopard by its light gray fur, which is spotted with black rings— perfect camouflage in the snow.

Snow leopards

**Its long tail helps to keep it warm.** When a snow leopard is tired, it curls up with its long tail around its neck like a scarf and goes to sleep. When it is on the move, its tail helps it balance as it leaps from rock to rock.

**Its big feet are like snowshoes.** A snow leopard has wide paws that help it stay on top of the snow. Their paws are covered with long hair so they don't slide on the ice.

A snow leopard attacks a mountain goat.

**What do they find to eat in the snowy mountains?** In summer, snow leopards hunt for prey in the high grassy pastures. They attack gorals and wild goats such as markhors. These animals also have thick, heavy coats. In winter, snow leopards move lower down the mountain. They sneak into the forests in search of wild sheep, boars, pheasants, and partridges. Even the huge yaks fear that their young may be attacked by a hungry snow leopard.

Yaks

**Snow leopards are an endangered species,** and it is illegal to hunt them. So many have been hunted for their fur that there are fewer than 1,000 left in the wild.

Markhor

Gorals

# Snub-nosed monkeys and moon bears live in the Himalayas of Asia.

Snub-nosed monkeys keep to the trees. They climb down to the ground only to eat and drink. They live in groups and roam around the forests looking for leaves. They also feed on fruit, buds, bamboo shoots, insects, eggs, and even birds. Snub-nosed monkeys have practically no nose. They have a thick, golden brown coat that protects them from the snow. They are also called rhinopithecus monkeys. Because they are rare and live in remote mountain regions, little is known about them.

**Keep out of the way of moon bears!** The people who live in the Himalayan mountains are terrified of coming face to face with a moon bear on a narrow path. These bears are easily provoked and will attack people and their horses. They live in forests in the high mountains, at about

A snub-nosed monkey

4,925 to 9,840 feet (1,500 to 3,000 m).
  These mountain dwellers are called moon bears because of the crescent-shaped patch of white fur on their chests.

**Moon bears are clever.** They are good swimmers and excellent tree climbers. When the weather is bad, they sleep in a sheltered place high in a tree. In winter, they gather grass and twigs to make a den in a sunny spot on the snow. There they rest and dry their fur.

**A family of bears**
Unlike other kinds of bears that like to live alone, the male moon bear lives with a female and sometimes with its cubs.

**Moon bears eat everything.** They are omnivorous. They feed on fruit and nuts as well as ants, larvae, small animals, and even decaying carcasses.

# Orangutans swing through the tropical rainforests of Asia.

**In the jungle you can't see the sky!** Liana creepers and the branches of enormous trees arch overhead to form a green canopy. Plants and trees grow together so closely in Borneo, Indonesia, that you need an ax to cut your way through the jungle. Flying frogs, squirrels, and lizards glide through the air. The orangutan spends most of its life in the trees.

Orangutans throw branches down at their enemies.

**Orangutans enjoy their food.** In the forests of Indonesia, they walk for hours in search of litchis, some wild figs, or a durian—a big, spiny, smelly fruit that they love. They only select the best—orangutans are fussy eaters.

**The male orangutan lives on his own.** But in the mating season, he broadcasts his presence to females for many miles around with a long, piercing scream. Males are twice as big as females, and the most dominant males have rolls of fat around their cheeks and foreheads to make them look bigger. Baby orangutans are small and delicate. They cling to their mother all the time to avoid getting lost in the jungle. They stay with her for a long time, maybe even for several years.

Orangutans are an endangered species.

They lean down very carefully to drink— they can't swim!

# Some primates live on the ground; others prefer the trees.

Gibbons swing through the trees . . .

. . . 100 feet (30 m) up . . .

. . . and can leap across a 26-foot (8 m) clearing in one bound.

**Who's up there in the treetops?** A gibbon, the acrobat of the trees! With its enormously long arms, it dangles like a trapeze artist and swings from tree to tree. But it can lose its balance and fall down.

Proboscis monkeys have long noses.

Gibbons live in many Asian forests.

Siamangs can blow up a sac of stretchy skin beneath their chin.

**Gibbons are very loving.**
A male and a female, or sometimes a male and two females, live with their young as a family group.

**Every morning they screech a noisy greeting across the jungle,** then the whole family sets out to look for food. They pick fruit, leaves, flowers, and buds. They catch insects and steal birds' eggs. In the afternoon they stop for a nap, and at sunset they return to their own territory to sleep.

**Female gibbons have a baby every two or three years.** Young gibbons stay with the family until they reach adulthood at about eight years old.

**Proboscis monkeys have big, droopy noses.** Sometimes their noses are so long they get in the way when they are feeding on leaves and fruits. Proboscis monkeys live in groups among the mangrove swamps of Borneo.

**Macaques are well-organized.** They don't squabble, and they work together to defend themselves. They spend a lot of time on the ground, walking single file in a long line. They groom each other to get rid of parasites and to relax.

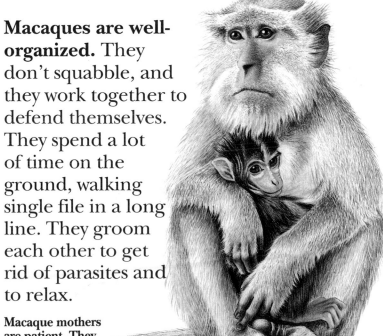

Macaque mothers are patient. They teach their babies everything.

# Tigers stalk silently through the jungle.

**Hunting and habitat loss threaten the tiger.** Even though tigers are in danger of extinction, people still hunt them. People want their bones and other body parts to use in Asian medicines. Unless threats to tigers can be stopped, the largest of all cats may become extinct.

About 100 years ago, there were 100,000 tigers in the world. Scientists estimate that about 6,000 tigers now remain in the wild.

**Ravenous and crafty**
A tiger eats about 33 pounds (15 kg) of meat a day. When it has killed its prey, it may drag the carcass several hundred yards to a sheltered place. If it cannot eat it all, it will cover the flesh with leaves or hide it underwater so that another meat-eater will not smell it. No tiger wants to have its food stolen!

# Tiger cubs must learn to hunt.

Tigers are the largest of all cats. They can weigh more than 551 pounds (250 kg).

Despite its size, a tiger creeps silently through the undergrowth, ready to pounce on deer, antelope, and rabbits.

**Tigers live alone until it is time to mate.** Then, the female spreads her strong-smelling urine all over her territory to

Look out, tiger! The elephant may charge you.

attract a male. For a few days, the tiger and tigress hunt together and share their prey. Then they mate. After this, the male often leaves. The cubs are born 100 days later in a den the mother makes.

**Tiger cubs learn to hunt as they play.** They love stalking each other and pouncing on their mother's tail. By the time they are six months old, they can catch birds. Then they begin to hunt with their mother. When they are two years old, they are ready to leave.

**A young tiger makes its own territory,** marking the border with its urine, scratching the ground, and slashing trees to let other tigers know they must keep away. It will defend its territory against other tigers.

## A tiger is constantly hunting

While tigers are skilled and powerful hunters, it is estimated that only one in 20 attacks on prey results in success. Tigers hunt more than they eat or sleep!

# Australia has many extraordinary animals.

Spiny anteaters and duck-billed platypuses are mammals, like sheep or goats, but they lay eggs! Kangaroos and koalas are marsupials that carry their babies in a pouch.

What's this animal hopping along like a big rabbit? It's called the greater rabbit-eared bandicoot.

**Kangaroos bound across the desert.** The largest kangaroos can jump about 33 feet (10 m) in a hop and travel as fast as 31 miles (50 km) per hour. Wallabies are the kangaroo's smaller cousins.

## Growing up in a pouch

When a kangaroo is born it is only about half an inch (1 cm) long. It's blind and helpless, but it crawls through its mother's fur and into her pouch where it sucks milk from her teat. As it grows bigger and stronger, it climbs in and out of her pouch. When it is eight months old, it leaves its cozy home. But a new baby will soon take its place in the pouch.

**At night the desert echoes with howls.** As one howl dies away, another follows. Dingoes howl to talk to each other. These wild dogs look like wolves and live in packs, hunting rabbits and small animals.

These devilish lizards only look dangerous. The shingle-backed lizard, about one and a half feet (45 cm) long, is really quite harmless. It has a piercing whistle, and it sticks out its blue tongue when it is attacked.

The frilled lizard also whistles if it's cornered and spreads out a fold of skin around its neck to appear fierce.

The moloch, or mountain devil, looks like a dragon, but it's actually no bigger than your hand. It eats ants.

Frilled lizard

# The duck-billed platypus is odd.

**Koalas only eat eucalyptus.** They eat more than 2.2 pounds (1 kg) of eucalyptus leaves a night. At mating time the male koala is fierce. It patrols its territory, ready to chase away other males. The female has one baby a year. She carries it in her pouch until it is six or seven months old. Then it moves around and clings onto her back.

The lyre bird spreads out its tail like a peacock.

Kookaburras are related to kingfishers.

Koalas

**The dawn chorus in Australia is unique.** Parrots and lorikeets come in every color. The kookaburra laughs, and the bellbird makes a ringing sound like a bell.

**What has an otter's body and a duck's head?** A duck-billed platypus. It eats crabs, larvae, and small fish. The female lays two or three eggs in a small burrow in the riverbank. They hatch in one or two weeks. The mother has no nipples but produces milk that seeps from her glands through her skin. The babies lap it up.

Duck-billed platypus

A dingo scans the desert, not noticing the moloch and shingle-backed lizard behind it.

# The animals on tropical islands are not seen anywhere else.

**Mouse lemur**

Madagascar is a large tropical island just off the southeast coast of Africa. It is the home of the lemur, ancestor to the monkey.

Islands like Madagascar, the Seychelles, the Antilles, and the Galapagos have a range of extraordinary reptiles and birds that attract visitors from all over the world.

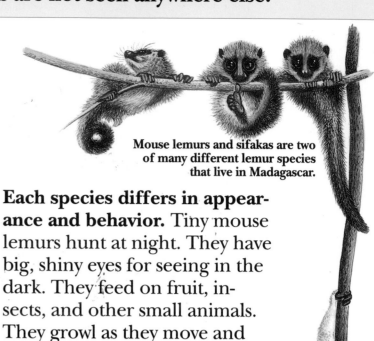

Mouse lemurs and sifakas are two of many different lemur species that live in Madagascar.

**Each species differs in appearance and behavior.** Tiny mouse lemurs hunt at night. They have big, shiny eyes for seeing in the dark. They feed on fruit, insects, and other small animals. They growl as they move and snap at any bird of prey that attacks them.

Sifakas are large, agile lemurs that jump from one tree trunk to another, feeding mostly in the daytime. They have scent glands beneath their chins and mark their territory by rubbing scent onto tree branches.

**The macaco lemur is endangered.** The male has thick, silky black fur and the female is reddish-orange. They spend a lot of time basking in the sun. They love bananas and mangoes and are so tame that they will take food straight from your hand.

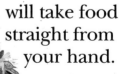

Aye-ayes are lemurs with amazingly long middle fingers. They grub out larvae from beneath the bark of trees.

**Turtles lay their eggs on land.** As the sun sets, you can watch the females crawling over the sand. They swim fast in water but move painfully slowly on land. Far up the beach, out of reach of the high tide, the female turtle digs a small hole. She lays about 100 eggs in it. She carefully covers the nest with sand and returns to the sea.

**Few baby turtles survive.** The eggs stay warm in the hot sand and hatch after two months. The tiny turtles instinctively start crawling back to sea. Seabirds hovering overhead dive down and eat most of them before they reach the water. Some species of turtle are endangered because people have killed too many of them for their meat, hides, and eggs.

# The largest animal in the world . . .

Whales and dolphins swim in the sea, but they are not fish. They come to the surface to breathe air and feed their babies milk. Whales are mammals called cetaceans—many are endangered.

Some species of whales feed on fish and squid, chewing them with their teeth. Most of the largest whales have no teeth at all.

**Sperm whales can stay underwater for an hour and a half!** They dive deeper than any other whale in their search for squid and fish. They can dive deeper than half a mile (1 km) to capture prey.

**Killer whales are expert hunters.** They swim in packs, their large dorsal fins slicing through the surface of the water. They attack sharks, seals, dolphins, and even other whales. They eat a huge amount, but they don't attack people.

The sperm whale is the largest toothed whale. Killer whales are not whales, but a sort of large dolphin. The beluga, also called the white whale, is dark gray when it is born but becomes white when it is about five years old.

Dolphins

Sperm whale

Killer whale

Beluga, or white whale

The narwhale has just one long tooth, like a horn, to defend itself.

## The blue whale is the largest and heaviest mammal ever!

Dolphins can swim very fast—up to 31 miles (50 km) per hour. They leap out of the water to take breaths of air.

Some are 98 feet (30 m) long and weigh as much as 30 elephants. Blue whales have no teeth. Instead, they have rows of horny plates called baleen, and so they are called baleen whales.

**Baleen whales swallow huge gulps of tiny plants and animals called plankton.** The food is filtered through the rows of baleen plates that hang down from the top of the whale's mouth.

Blue whales eat 2,205 pounds (1,000 kg) of tiny animals in a single meal. The whales below are all baleen whales.

Whales breathe in through two nostrils, or blowholes, on top of their heads. But first they blow out a cloud of steamy, stale air!

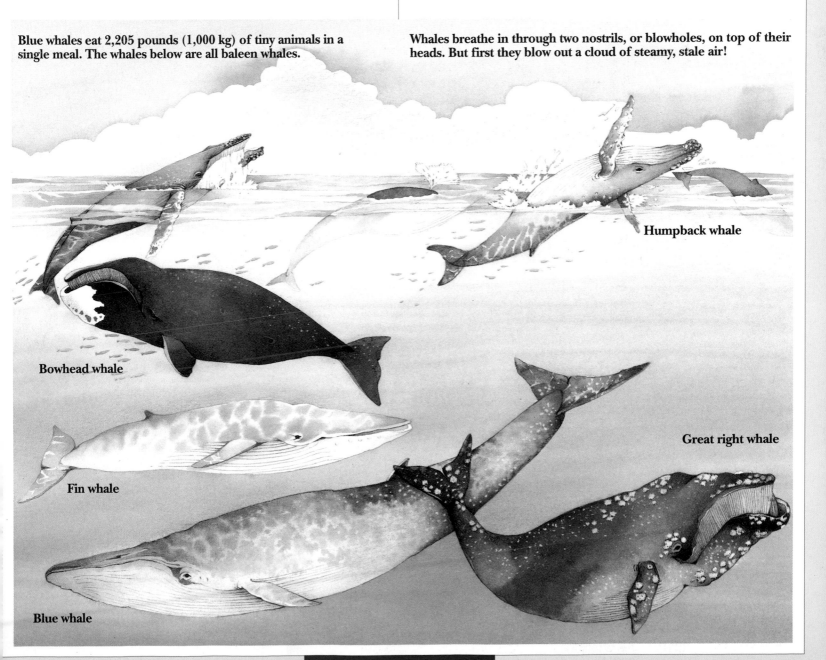

Humpback whale

Bowhead whale

Great right whale

Fin whale

Blue whale

# The largest baby on our planet

A dolphin calf is born.

It rides on its mother's back.

The mother dolphin suckles her calf for 16 months.

**A newborn blue whale weighs 11,000 pounds** (5 metric tons) and is 23 feet (7 m) long. Its mother has to coax the calf to the surface to take its first vital breaths of air, but it suckles underwater.

The calf drinks about 119 gallons (450 L) of its mother's milk a day.

The whale calf doubles its birth weight in a week, so it puts on almost 10 pounds (4.5 kg) every hour! The baby is born in warm seas near the equator. Before it can go to the cold polar seas, a trip that takes several months, it must build up a thick layer of fatty blubber.

The mother whale protects her calf. She will risk her own life to save it from attack.

# Whales and dolphins have their own language.

**Whales and dolphins are very sociable** and live in family groups called schools. Sometimes several hundred live together with one animal acting as leader.

**Why do they leap out of the water?** To raise the alarm, to keep in contact in rough seas, or sometimes to attract females. The young jump just for fun!

**Dolphins are very intelligent.** Divers can train dolphins to help fetch objects from the ocean bed, and they are quick to learn tricks based on their natural movements. Have you seen them balancing

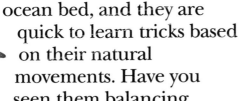

A dolphin

upright on their tails and leaping through hoops? Tame killer whales and dolphins perform in zoos and aquariums. These creatures are fun to watch, but they don't live long in captivity.

**Whistles, groans, chirps, and clicks . . .** These are the sounds whales and dolphins use to communicate with each other. They make other sounds as well, too high pitched for humans to hear. Dolphins and toothed whales have poor eyesight, but they have excellent hearing. Like bats, they use high-pitched sounds to detect if anything is in their way. The returning echoes tell them the shape of the object and also how far away it is.

Sea lions

**Many other mammals live in the sea.** Seals, sea lions, and walruses are called pinnipeds. They spend only part of their lives on land or on ice floes. Their skin is covered with short, sleek fur, and they hunt fish, crabs, shellfish, and seabirds. They can stay underwater for up to 20 minutes.

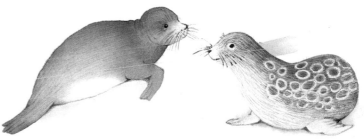

The monk seal lives in the Mediterranean Sea.

The smallest seal is the ringed seal.

The largest pinniped is the elephant seal. It can weigh 8,818 pounds (4 metric tons) and can measure nearly 16.4 feet (7 m) from nose to tail.

The gray seal lives off the coasts of Britain.

The male elephant seal can inflate his nose like a trunk.

**How can you tell a sea lion from a seal?** A sea lion's ears are on the outside of its head. A seal's are not.

Host fish live wherever they can feed on plankton. The types of fish found in an area vary depending on the temperature of the water and the kind of plants growing there. Coral reefs teem with brilliantly colored clownfish, damselfish, and angelfish. We still have much to learn about the life in the deep seas.

**A shark's dorsal fin slices through the water** and keeps the shark steady. It is a terrifying sight and perhaps the only sign that the shark is there. The shark uses its other fins to help it turn.

**Sharks are fast, silent hunters.** Their powerful tails propel them forward through the water. Some sharks eat plankton, but most catch fish, squid, and shellfish.

The great white shark attacks turtles, seabirds, and even other sharks, leaping out of the water to snatch seals and sea lions. It tears them apart with its rows of terrible teeth. When a tooth wears out, a new one replaces it. A shark goes through thousands of teeth in its life.

Manta rays are the largest flat fish. They can be 23 feet (7 m) wide and weigh more than 4,410 pounds (2,000 kg). They flap their fins while swimming and look as if they are flying under the water.

Black tip
reef shark

Tiger shark

Marlin

Manta ray

# Intriguing facts, activities, games, a quiz, a glossary, and books to read, followed by the index

## ■ Did you know?

**The elephant's earliest ancestor was the moeritherium,** which lived more than 60 million years ago. Slowly, generation by generation, its descendants, which included the dinotherium and the mastodon, grew bigger and bigger. Their noses gradually grew longer, until they finally developed into trunks. Two of their upper teeth grew into tusks.

**Dinotherium**

**Mastodon**

**Mammoths were hairy cousins of the elephant.** They first appeared on Earth 10 million years ago. The complete, frozen bodies of some ancient mammoths have been found in the Arctic ice.

**Lions and elephants once roamed across what is now the Sahara Desert.** Even as recently as 2,000 years ago, North Africa had more rain and more plants and trees than it has now.

**Indian elephants are different from African elephants.** Indian elephants have smaller ears and a rounder head than their African cousins. They live in the dense, steamy tropical forests of southern Asia.

### Helpful and strong
People in India traditionally use the intelligence and strength of female elephants to help them with hard and heavy work. Older elephants help to teach younger ones how to do the work.

**Elephants live to a great age.** They usually die of hunger when they are about 50 to 60 years old. By then their teeth have worn away.

In Asia, only male elephants have visible tusks.

In India, each working elephant has its own keeper, or mahout, who always looks after it.

### Elephant school
The elephant learns how to carry its master and to understand commands. Later, it learns how to lift heavier and heavier tree trunks. When it's finished learning, it's put to work in the forest where the land is too swampy for bulldozers.

**Black rhinos and white rhinos are really the same color!** Only the shape of their mouth is different. White rhinos have large, straight mouths for grazing on grass. Black rhinos have pointed mouths for browsing on leaves.

**"What a little monkey you are!"** When people say that, they mean you are being sassy and naughty. But when monkeys or apes call out and jump up and down, clapping their hands, they aren't fooling around—they are talking to each other and showing each other whether they are happy, friendly, or angry.

**Apes have long arms**—longer than their legs. Unlike monkeys, they have no tail. Apes are humans' closest relatives.

**Humans, monkeys, apes, and lemurs belong to the same family: the primates.** They all have hands that can grip and eyes that can see color and measure distance. Monkeys and apes have feet that can grip too. They use them to grab and hold branches.

## ■ Did you know?

**Red pandas** live in China and Nepal. They are about the size and shape of a pet cat. The fur on their back

is thick and red, and their belly is black. There are more red pandas than giant pandas, but they are shy and not often seen. They live in forests and use their claws to climb trees. They eat bamboo shoots and fruit, varying their diet with insects, eggs, and small birds.

**In ancient Egypt, people worshipped crocodiles as gods.** In the pharaohs' time, a city—named Crocodilopolis—was built in their honor. Priests put gold bracelets on crocodiles' arms and fed them cakes and honey.

**What are "crocodile tears"?** People say this to mean "pretend crying" because crocodiles have tears in their eyes only if they yawn or are washing sea salt from their eyes.

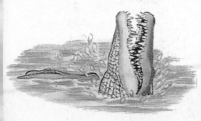

**People used to capture bears and teach them tricks.** They would travel from town to town with a bear show. Bears are intelligent and learn quickly, but don't adapt well to being in captivity.

**Sun bears** love to sunbathe! They have sleek fur like a seal, and the palms of their paws are hairless to help them cling to palm trees. They eat coconuts and sugarcane and lie on a branch basking in the hot sun. They do not need to hibernate.

They come from Malaysia and are the smallest of all bears. They weigh less than 143 pounds (65 kg) and are only about three feet (1 m) long.

**Nile crocodile**

**Crocodiles are becoming rare.** They have been hunted for their skins, which are valuable. They are now protected and many live in reserves.

**Central American caiman**

Skins used for expensive handbags, belts, and shoes should not come from wild crocodiles, caimans, gavials, or alligators but from crocodiles raised on special farms.

## ■ Did you know?

**Wild cats have beautiful, patterned fur** which helps them hide while they stalk their prey. Leopards and lynx have dappled fur; tigers have stripes. They can blend into their surroundings, unheard and unseen, until they're ready to pounce. Their strong muscles and powerful jaws enable them to kill prey twice their own size. Cats kill what they need to eat. Then they rest.

**Why do cats have green eyes?** They have special mirror-like reflectors at the back of their eyeballs that catch the light and reflect it forward.

**Cats have enemies too.** They are careful to avoid elephants, which may charge them and trample them to death, particularly if the adults are protecting baby elephants. Cats watch out for crocodiles when they go to the water to drink, and they fear snakes, which might spit poison at them or squeeze them to stop their breathing. But the big cats' greatest enemies are people who hunt them for their fur.

In the dry savanna, lions hide in the grass to wait for antelope and giraffes.

**Wildlife alert!** The snow leopard, the Bengal tiger, and almost all the big cats are in danger of dying out. Lions are usually safe from hunters because their fur is not considered beautiful, but their habitats are under threat from development by humans.

**Lions are the only cats that live in family groups.** The lionesses hunt together and bring back food for the male lions and cubs. Although the male lions may seem lazy, their job is to protect the whole family.

**Have you ever seen an eagle attacking its prey?** It hovers in the sky with its wings outstretched. Then, it sees a rat. Suddenly it dives toward the ground and drops onto its prey. The bird seizes its prey in its talons and soars into the sky again. The eagle can carry heavy prey up to the mountain peaks where it has its aerie, or nest.

A leopard sometimes hides in a tree so it can drop down on its unsuspecting prey.

# ■ Quiz

Can you answer these questions? The answers are at the bottom of this page.

**1. Chimps like to eat**
a. grass.
b. mice.
c. termites.

**2. Which bear does not sleep through the winter?**
a. brown bear
b. black bear
c. sun bear

**3. Which is the largest penguin?**
a. royal penguin
b. emperor penguin
c. pygmy penguin

**4. Which bird does not build a nest?**
a. ostrich
b. eagle
c. emperor penguin

**5. How much does a newborn polar bear cub weigh?**
a. one and a half pounds (700 grams)
b. four pounds (1.5 kg)
c. 11 pounds (5 kg)

**6. Which of these bears is the largest?**
a. sun bear
b. spectacled bear
c. polar bear

**7. Which of these bears is the smallest?**
a. moon bear
b. brown bear
c. sun bear

**8. Which of these cats is the largest?**
a. ocelot
b. lion
c. Siberian tiger

**9. Which bird helps elephants to get rid of their parasites?**
a. plover
b. tickbird
c. ibis

**10. What irritates rhinos most?**
a. insects
b. crocodiles
c. lions

# ■ True or false?

1. Elephants' trunks have no bones.
2. Baby elephants suck their trunks.
3. There are elephant cemeteries.
4. Elephants eat almost all day long.
5. African elephants cannot be trained.
6. Elephants walk in a long line, each holding the tail of the one in front.
7. You can tell how old an elephant is by looking at its teeth.
8. Elephants have thick, tough skin.

**Answers**

**Quiz**
1 c, 2 c, 3 b, 4 c, 5 a, 6 c, 7 b, 8 c, 9 b, 10 a

**True or false**
1. True. 2. True (just like some kids do when they suck their thumb). 3. False (It is a legend. People thought it was true because they found the carcasses of a whole herd that had gotten stuck in a swamp.). 4. True. 5. False (but they are more difficult to train than Indian elephants). 6. True. 7. True. 8. False.

# ■ Who's who?

Serval

Albino tiger

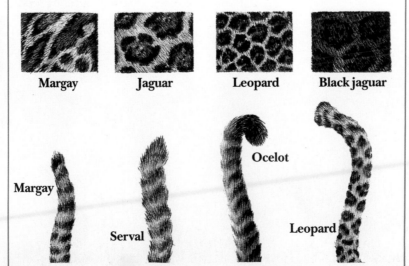
Margay    Jaguar    Leopard    Black jaguar

Pampas cat    Ocelot

Jaguar
Pampas cat

Margay    Serval    Ocelot    Leopard

Albino tiger
Black jaguar

## ■ Did you know?

**Sloth bears** love eating termites and will break into their nests and lick out the insects with their tongues. The terrible noise they make doing this can be heard 219 yards (200 m) away, making them easy prey for hunters.

**Whales are found in oceans all over the world.** In summer, some migrate to the colder oceans near the North and South poles where there is plenty of food. In winter, they move into warmer waters closer to the equator. There they find a mate and give birth to their young.

**Killer whales have huge appetites.** Scientists once found the remains of 11 seals and 13 porpoises in the stomach of a whale! Killer whales prey on sharks, seals, dolphins, and birds, as well as on squid and fish. A group of killer whales will even attack a large whale, which does not stand a chance against these agile killers with their rows of fearsome teeth. But don't worry, killer whales do not attack people.

A 19th-century whaling ship

**Save the whales!** Until a few hundred years ago, many whales of all kinds lived in the sea. Then people started killing too many of them. There are now so few of some species that they are almost extinct. In the 1980s, whaling was banned in most countries, and whale populations have started to grow again. But a few countries still allow whaling. Japan, for instance, allows whaling for scientific purposes only.

**Why do people hunt whales?** In the past, the body of a whale provided many things humans found useful. The blubber was melted down to provide oil.

A catcher ship drags its prey alongside.

Before electricity, whale oil was used as fuel in lamps. It was also used to make margarine, soap, cosmetic oil, and shoe polish. Baleen was used for umbrella spokes.

This factory ship hoists the whale on board, where it is tied to the deck.

**Today, people no longer need whale oil** because they have electricity. We now have alternative products for everything people once got from whales. In Japan, whale meat was once cheap, but now it is a luxury because most whale hunting is banned and the sale of whale products is illegal.

Carving on a sperm whale's tooth

## Did you know?

Walruses are cousins of the seal. They have two huge tusks that they use to dig for shellfish on the sea bottom and to haul themselves onto ice floes.

**Walruses push their bellies off of the ground and walk** using their flippers as legs when they are on land.

The dorsal fin of a killer whale

The tail of a blue whale

**Whales cannot survive out of water.** Although they breathe air, they cannot live very long on land. Without water to support them, the weight of their body crushes them to death.

**Krill are tiny shrimps** that blue whales and other baleen whales love to eat. But people have started fishing krill too. If people catch too many, there won't be enough for the whales.

**Some whales travel thousands of miles for their food.** Krill and plankton thrive in cold, icy waters. Whales swim to the Antarctic or Arctic in summer to feed on them.

**The blue whale** is the world's largest animal. Some are about 100 feet (30 m) long—the length of four buses parked one behind the other.

Skeleton of a fin whale

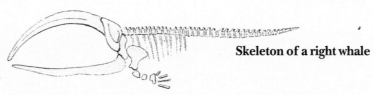

Skeleton of a right whale

**Many animals have already become extinct.**
Dinosaurs, mammoths, and many other animals became extinct thousands of years ago. And in the last few hundred years, many animals have become extinct because people have hunted them. They include 17 kinds of bears; five kinds of wolves and foxes; four kinds of cats; 10 kinds of cattle, sheep, goats, and antelope; and three kinds of deer. Many of these animals were killed for their fur, wool, or skins.

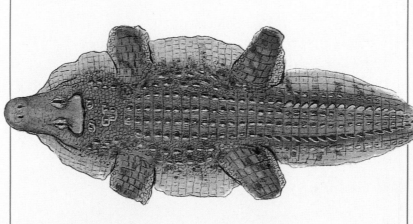

These products may be beautiful or fashionable—but crocodile skin looks better on crocodiles!

**Some animals thrive alongside people!** Mice, rats, pigeons, and cockroaches are just a few of the animals that live off of humans' food and trash. Foxes, gray squirrels, and raccoons are becoming common city dwellers.

**Some unexpected guests**
You might be surprised by the animals you see in some cities.

In India, sacred cows wander about the streets.

In Florida, alligators have been found in swimming pools. People drained the marshes where the alligators lived and built on them. Now the alligators are breeding in the sewers.

In Turkey, eagles live in the tops of old houses.

In Australia, opossums come into towns and cities looking for trash.
Elk sometimes stray into Moscow, Russia, and Helsinki, Finland.

## ■ Glossary

**Aerie:** a bird's nest, built on a high place.

**Big cat:** large member of the cat family. Jaguars, leopards, lions, tigers, and ocelots are all big cats.
**Browse:** to feed on leaves, twigs, bark, and shoots of trees and bushes.

**Camouflage:** the color and patterns of an animal's skin or fur that help it blend into its surroundings.
**Carcass:** the dead body or remains of an animal, especially one that has been killed for food.
**Clutch:** a group of eggs that are incubated and hatch together.
**Coniferous:** kinds of trees, many with needles, that produce seed cones.

**Domesticated:** something people have tamed.
**Dominant:** ruling or leading. The strongest member of a group often dominates the rest.

**Dorsal:** situated on the back. Whales, dolphins, and fish have dorsal fins to keep them from rolling in the water.
**Endangered:** in danger or threatened. When a whole

species of plant or animal is threatened with extinction, it is said to be an endangered species.
**Equator:** an imaginary line around the middle of Earth.
**Evaporate:** to change from a liquid to a vapor or gas. When a liquid evaporates, it takes heat from its surroundings and cools them down.
**Extinct:** no longer existing. When all the plants or animals in a particular species have died, the species is said to be extinct.

**Gland:** part of the body that produces a special substance, such as hormones or a strong-smelling liquid.
**Graze:** to feed mainly on grass.

**Habitat:** the natural home of a particular plant or animal.

**Ice floe:** a lump of floating ice.
**Incubate:** to keep eggs warm until the young inside are ready to hatch. Most birds incubate their eggs by sitting on them.

**Larva:** an early stage in the life cycle of an insect or other animal that will look different when it becomes an adult. Caterpillars, for example, grow into moths or butterflies.
**Liana creeper:** a plant with spreading stems.
**Lyre:** an old musical instrument that resembles a harp.

**Mammal:** member of a group of animals that feed their babies on milk the mother produces. Most mammals have hair and give birth to live young.
**Mangrove:** tropical trees that grow in swampy ground at the mouth of rivers.
**Marsupial:** an animal group in which the female has a pouch to carry her young before they are fully developed.

**Mate:** when a male and female come together to produce young.
**Migrate:** to move from place to place according to the season of the year.
**Minerals:** chemicals that animals need to eat to be healthy.
**Muzzle:** projecting part of an animal's face that includes mouth and nose.

**Nature reserve:** area of land in which farming is limited and animals are protected; it can also be called a game reserve or a wildlife reserve.
**Nocturnal:** to be more active at night.

**Omnivore:** an animal that eats plants and animals.
**Oxygen:** a gas that supports life on Earth. All living things breathe oxygen.
**Pack ice:** area of ice and water with many ice floes.

**Parasite:** plant or animal that lives and feeds on a host plant or animal.
**Plankton:** tiny plants and animals drifting in the sea.
**Prairie:** large area of natural grassland in North America.
**Predator:** an animal that hunts other animals for food.

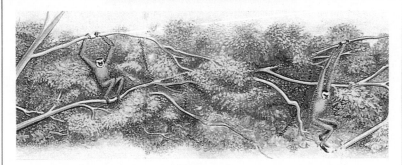

**Prey:** an animal that is hunted for food.
**Protected species:** a kind of animal or plant that you cannot harm or kill without legal permission.

**Rainforest:** tropical forest that grows where it is hot and there is plenty of rain all year round.
**Reptile:** a large group of animals that includes snakes, turtles, lizards, and crocodiles. Reptiles are covered with scales and rely on the sun's heat to warm their bodies.

**Rodent:** a small mammal with large gnawing teeth. Mice and squirrels are rodents.

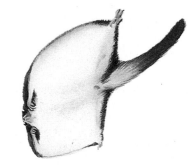

**Savanna:** area of tropical grassland in South America, Africa, or Australia.
**Species:** group of animals whose members are closely related and can breed with each other.
**Suckle:** to drink milk from the mother. Mammal babies suckle from their mother.

**Termite:** a tropical insect that lives in large groups.

**Territory:** area where an animal hunts or feeds.
**Ton:** 2,000 pounds. A metric ton is 1,000 kilograms, or 2,205 pounds.
**Tropics:** areas on each side of the equator where the weather is always hot and often very wet.

**Water hole:** shallow pond, often in a dry riverbed, where animals come to drink.

Here is a list of other books to read to find out more about exotic animals. Visit your library or a local bookstore to find still more titles.

*African Elephants: Giants of the Land*
by Dorothy Hinshaw Patent
  (Holiday House, 1991).

*Amazing Bears*
by Theresa Greenaway
  (Alfred A. Knopf, 1992).

*Amazing Mammals*
by Alexandra Parsons
  (Alfred A. Knopf, 1990).

*Arctic and Antarctic*
by Barbara Taylor
  (Alfred A. Knopf, 1995).

*Atlas of the Rain Forests*
by Anna Lewington (Raintree Steck-Vaughn Publishers, 1997).

*Birds: How to Watch and Understand the Fascinating World of Birds*
by Jill Bailey
  (Dorling Kindersley, 1992).

*Can We Save Them?*
by David Dobson
  (Charlesbridge, 1997).

*Children's Guide to Endangered Animals*
by Roger Few (Macmillan, 1993).

*The Crocodile Family Book*
by Mark Deeble
  (North-South Books, 1993).

*Endangered Mammals of North America*
by Victoria Sherrow
  (Twenty-First Century Books, 1995).

*Endangered!: Elephants*
by Amanda Harman
  (Benchmark Books, 1996).

*Endangered!: Whales*
by Amanda Harman
  (Benchmark Books, 1996).

*Ever Heard of an Aardwolf?*
*A Miscellany of Uncommon Animals*
  by Madeline Moser
  (Harcourt Brace and Company, 1996).

*Extremely Weird Mammals*
by Sarah Lovett (Davidson Titles, 1993).

*Fish*
by Edward Ricciuti
(Blackbirch Press, 1993).

*Life Cycle of a Dozen Diverse Creatures*
by Paul Fleisher
(The Millbrook Press, 1996).

*Lion*
by Caroline Arnold
(Morrow Junior Books, 1995).

*1000 Facts About Wild Animals*
by Moira Butterfield (Scholastic, 1992).

*Ostriches and Other Flightless Birds*
by Caroline Arnold
(Carolrhoda Books, 1990).

*Saving Endangered Mammals: A Field Guide to Some of the Earth's Rarest Animals*
by Thane Maynard
(Franklin Watts, 1992).

*The Snake Book*
by Frank Greenaway
(Dorling Kindersley Publishing, 1997).

*Strange Creatures*
by David Peters
(Morrow Junior Books, 1992).

*Whales and Dolphins*
by Steve Parker
(Sierra Club Books for Children, 1992).

*Who Comes to the Water Hole?*
by Colleen Stanley Bare
(Cobblehill Books, 1991).

*Will We Miss Them?*
Endangered Species by Alexandra Wright
(Charlesbridge Publishing, 1992).

Also check out Creative Education's *Zoobooks* series for many of the animals listed in this book, and Creative's *Images* series for books on the rainforest, Antarctica, oceans, islands, coral reefs, and more.

The entries in **bold** refer to whole chapters on the subject.